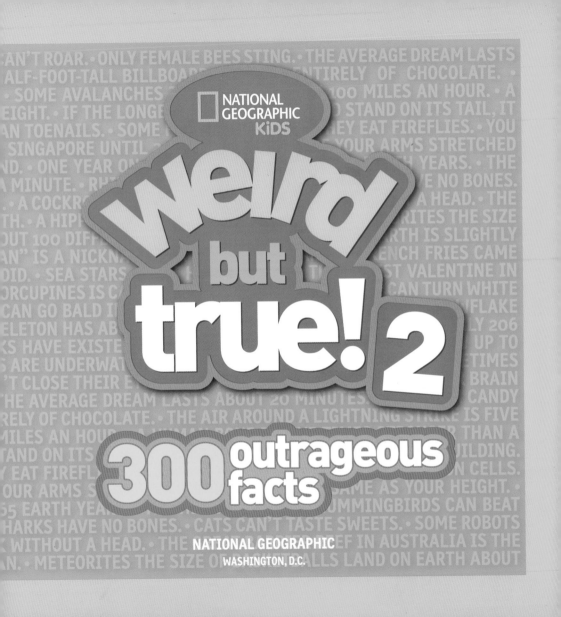

A bottlenose dolphin has a bigger **brain** than a human.

Snow leopards can't

roar.

A BRITISH JEWELER MADE A **TEA BAG** DECORATED WITH **280** DIAMONDS—IT WAS WORTH **£7,500!** (ABOUT $12,000)

ONLY FEMALE BEES STING.

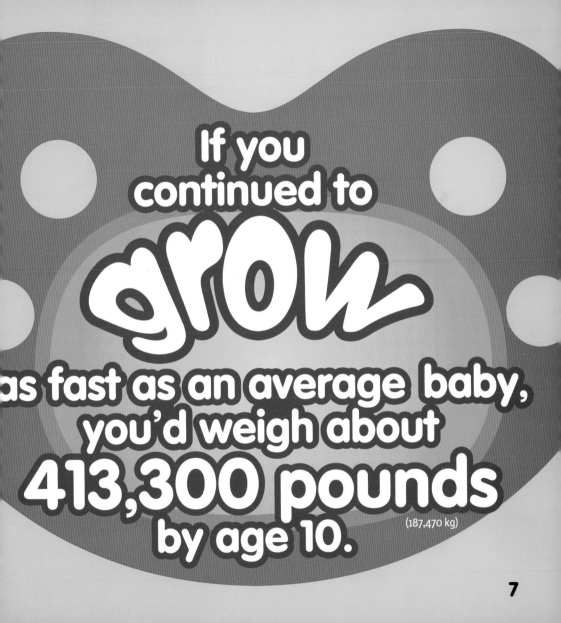

If you continued to **grow** as fast as an average baby, you'd weigh about **413,300 pounds** by age 10. (187,470 kg)

A BRITISH **CANDY-MAKER** ONCE CREATED A **NINE-AND-A-HALF-FOOT-TALL** (2.9 m) BILLBOARD MADE ENTIRELY OF **CHOCOLATE.**

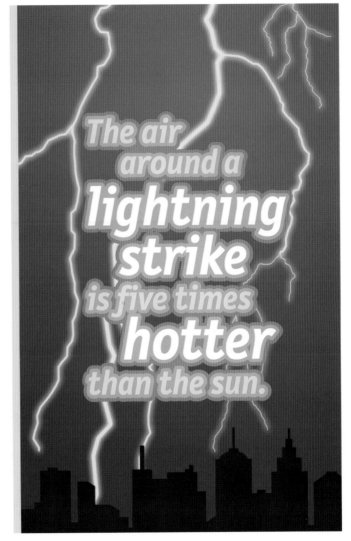

The air around a **lightning strike** *is five times* **hotter** *than the sun.*

Some avalanches travel more than 100 miles an hour.

(161 km)

A HUMAN BONE IS FIVE TIMES STRONGER THAN A PIECE OF STEEL OF THE SAME WEIGHT.

THE LONGEST RAW EGG TOSS WAS 107 YARDS. (98 m)

100 YARDS LONG (91 m)

THE DOTS ON DICE ARE CALLED PIPS.

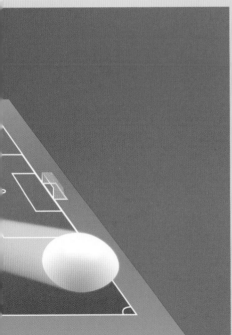

IF THE LONGEST **BLUE WHALE** COULD STAND ON ITS **TAIL,** IT WOULD BE AS **TALL** AS A TEN-STORY BUILDING.

Bats have thumbs.

ROCKETS MUST TRAVEL

AT LEAST **25,000 MILES** AN HOUR (40,234 km) TO **ESCAPE EARTH'S GRAVITY.**

There have been at least four major ice ages.

A chameleon's tongue can be as long as its body.

Christopher Columbus mistook a manatee for a mermaid.

Light travels *faster* than sound.

A newborn puppy can take up to **two months to** start wagging its tail.

Popcorn can pop up to three feet into the air. (0.9 m)

The **London Bridge** that kept **falling down** is now in Arizona in the United States.

A *ZEPTOSECOND* IS ONE-BILLIONTH OF A TRILLIONTH OF A SECOND.

NOTHING CAN ESCAPE FROM A BLACK HOLE.

AN AMERICAN MAN COOKED **427 OMELETS** IN 30 MINUTES.

Some butterflies' **ears** are on their **wings.**

Fingernails grow faster than toenails.

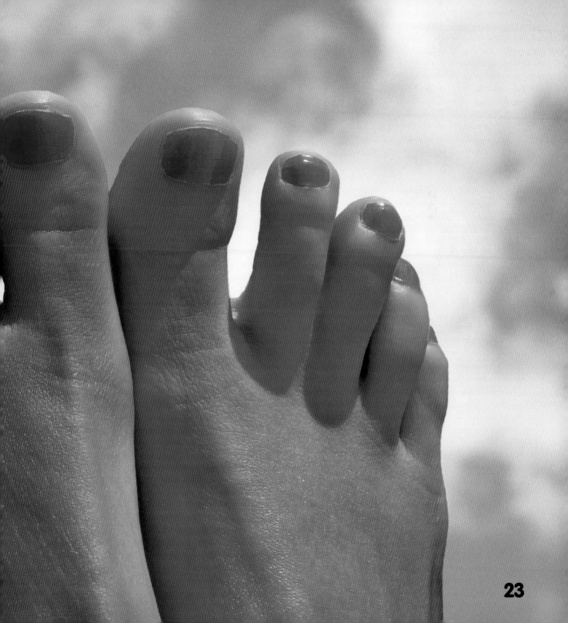

23

A camel can drink 500 cups (118 L) of water in ten minutes.

Gelotology is the study of laughter.

A supermarket in South Africa created a **pizza** that was **122 feet,** 8 inches across (37.4 m) and weighed as much as two male African elephants.

IF YOU TRAVELED AT THE SPEED OF LIGHT, YOU COULD REACH PLUTO IN JUST FOUR HOURS.

SOME FROGS GLOW WHEN THEY EAT FIREFLIES.

MEN GET THE HICCUPS MORE OFTEN THAN WOMEN DO.

A *JIFFY* is one-hundredth of a second.

THE WORLD'S TALLEST WATERFALL, CALLED ANGEL FALLS, IS TALLER THAN FIVE WASHINGTON MONUMENTS STACKED UP.

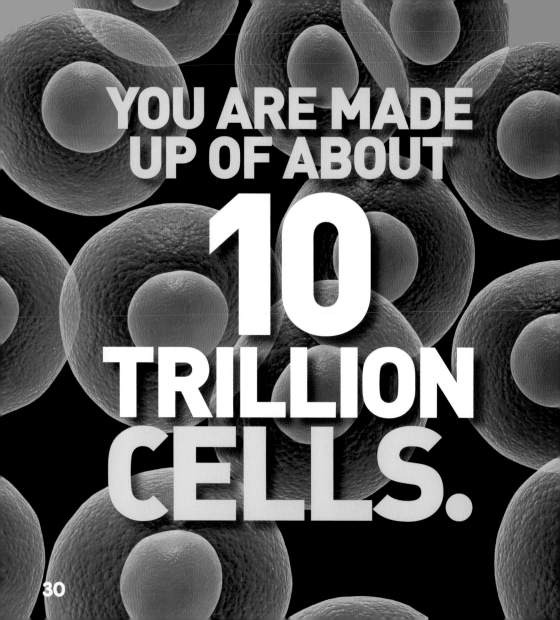

YOU ARE MADE
UP OF ABOUT

10
TRILLION
CELLS.

CHEWING GUM was banned in Singapore until 2004.

THE WORLD'S FIRST HANDHELD MOBILE PHONE COST $3,995.

The length of your arms stretched out is about equal to your height.

YOUR BRAIN IS SOMETIMES MORE ACTIVE WHEN YOU SLEEP THAN WHEN YOU'RE AWAKE.

A 95-mile-long underground river flows beneath Mexico.

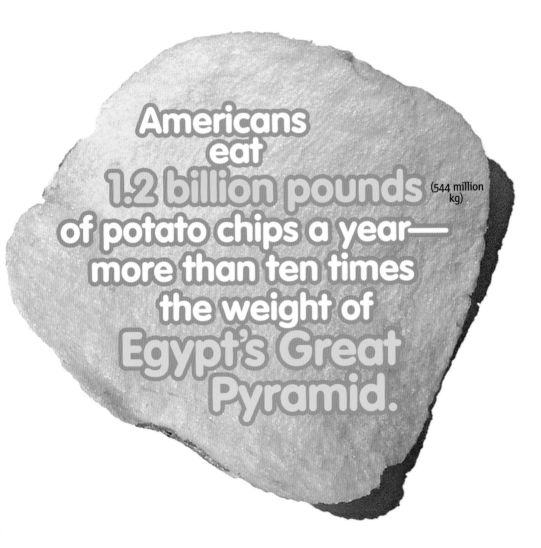

Americans eat 1.2 billion pounds (544 million kg) of potato chips a year—more than ten times the weight of Egypt's Great Pyramid.

DINOSAUR
BONES
WERE MISTAKEN FOR
DRAGON BONES
WHEN THEY WERE DISCOVERED MORE THAN
2,000 YEARS AGO.

NEWBORN BABIES ARE
COLOR-BLIND.

A 5,000-year-old piece of chewing gum was discovered in Finland.

THE WORLD'S **TALLEST TREE** —IS— **379.1 FEET** (115.6 m) **TALL,** ABOUT AS HIGH AS **188 SCHOOL DESKS STACKED UP.**

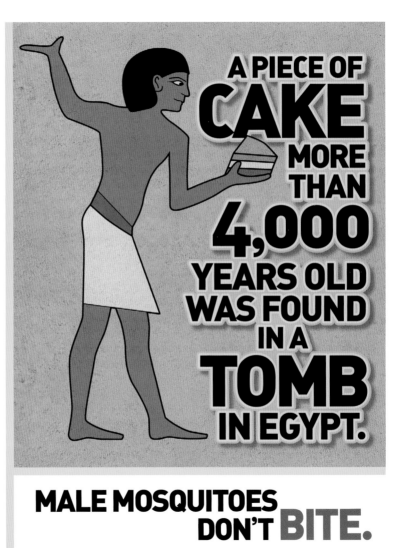

A PIECE OF **CAKE** MORE THAN **4,000** YEARS OLD WAS FOUND IN A **TOMB** IN EGYPT.

MALE MOSQUITOES DON'T BITE.

One year on **Neptune** lasts about **165 Earth years.**

ASTRONAUT **NEIL** ARMSTRONG LEFT HIS **SPACE BOOTS** ON THE **MOON.**

THE **FIRST** MICROWAVE **OVEN** WAS ALMOST AS **TALL** AS A REFRIGERATOR.

Some spiders eat their own webs.

There are about 16 million thunderstorms on Earth every year.

The planet Mercury is made mostly of iron.

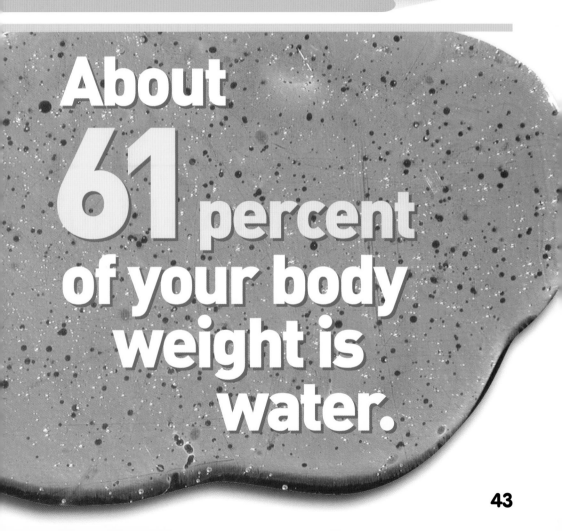

About **61** percent of your body weight is water.

THE HEARTS
OF SOME
HUMMINGBIRDS
CAN BEAT FASTER THAN

1,000

TIMES A MINUTE.

The ancient
Aztecs used cacao
(cocoa) beans
as money.

Rhinoceroses don't sweat.

A hill in New Zealand is named
Taumatawhakatangihangakoauau

IT'S POSSIBLE TO SMELL SCENTS IN DREAMS.

mateapokaiwhenuakitanatahu.

THE
GREAT
BARRIER
REEF
IN
AUSTRALIA
IS THE
BIGGEST
LIVING
STRUCTURE
ON EARTH.

You can tell the age of some fish by counting the rings on their scales.

Bloodhounds can follow a scent that is **four** days old.

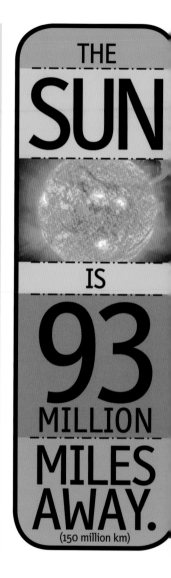

THE

SUN

IS

93
MILLION
MILES
AWAY.
(150 million km)

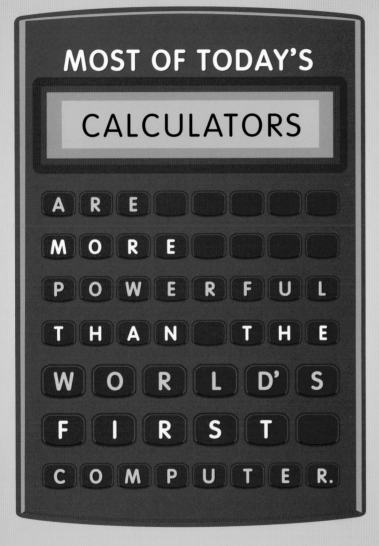

MOST OF TODAY'S

CALCULATORS

ARE MORE POWERFUL THAN THE WORLD'S FIRST COMPUTER.

ANIMALS THAT LAY EGGS DON'T HAVE BELLY BUTTONS.

A tiger's stripes are different on the left and right sides of its body.

The **first email was sent** in **1971.**

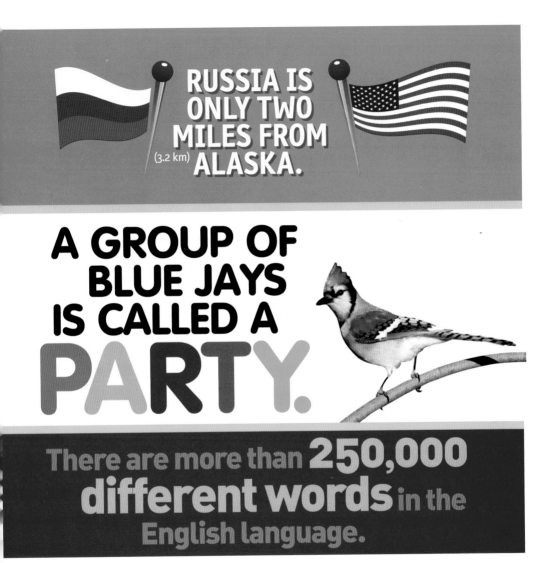

RUSSIA IS ONLY TWO MILES FROM ALASKA.
(3.2 km)

A GROUP OF BLUE JAYS IS CALLED A PARTY.

There are more than 250,000 different words in the English language.

SHARKS HAVE NO BONES.

CATS CAN'T TASTE SWEETS.

Some robots can identify different cheeses.

A COCKROACH CAN LIVE FOR OVER A **WEEK** WITHOUT A HEAD.

Earth's core is about the same size as the planet Mars.

Thousands of tiny earthquakes happen every day.

THE SAHARA
DESERT
IS LARGER
THAN
AUSTRALIA.

Venus
is the
hottest
planet in
our
solar system.

LIONS
SPEND ABOUT
20 HOURS A DAY
RESTING.

A TIGER
can eat
more than
80
pounds
(36 kg)
# of meat
in one sitting.

Most **people** spend about **five years** of their **lives** eating.

METEORITES THE SIZE OF BASKETBALLS LAND ON EARTH ABOUT ONCE A MONTH.

A HIPPO CAN RUN AS FAST AS *A HUMAN.*

A man **hiccuped** for 68 years straight.

NIGHTTIME RAINBOWS ARE CALLED MOONBOWS.

Enough whipped topping is manufactured every year to crisscross the United States more than 5 times.

75% of all animals are insects.

THE ✈
WINGSPAN OF A
747
IS
LONGER
THAN THE
WRIGHT BROTHERS'
FIRST FLIGHT.

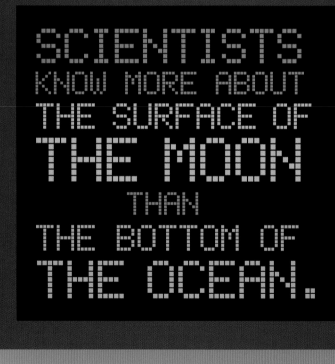

SCIENTISTS KNOW MORE ABOUT THE SURFACE OF THE MOON THAN THE BOTTOM OF THE OCEAN.

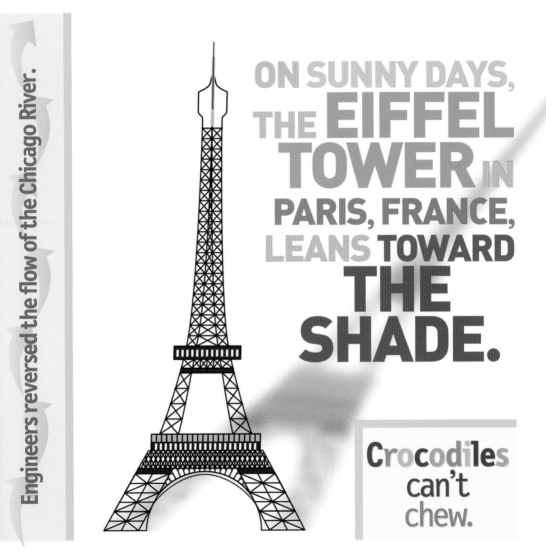

Engineers reversed the flow of the Chicago River.

ON SUNNY DAYS, THE **EIFFEL TOWER** IN **PARIS, FRANCE,** LEANS **TOWARD THE SHADE.**

Crocodiles can't chew.

63

64

A dog can make about

different facial expressions.

The Earth is slightly pear-shaped.

A zebra's skin is black; only its fur is striped.

A TROPICAL **ANT** CAN SNAP ITS JAWS TOGETHER AT A SPEED OF 145 MILES AN HOUR, (233 km) FASTER THAN ANY OTHER ANIMAL!

It takes the average 10-year-old kid

about 20 minutes to fall asleep.

MOUNT EVEREST GROWS MORE THAN ONE-EIGHTH OF AN INCH (3 mm) EACH YEAR.

1/8 inch

0 mm
10
20
30
40

"Old man" is a nickname for a male **kangaroo.**

One million seconds **is 11** days, **13** hours, 46 minutes, and 40 seconds.

The brighter the star, the **shorter** its life span.

French fries came fro

Belgium, not France.

GRAVITY PULLS UP DOWN AND SIDEWAYS AT THE CENTER OF THE EARTH.

THERE ARE MORE TV SETS IN THE UNITED STATES THAN THERE ARE PEOPLE IN THE UNITED KINGDOM.

WHEN YOU SEE LIGHTNING, IT'S TRAVELING AT ABOUT

227 MILLION MILES AN HOUR.
(365 million km)

A **volcano** in Italy has been erupting for 2,000 years.

TURTLES LIVED ON EARTH BEFORE DINOSAURS DID.

Queen Margherita of Savoy ordered the first pizza delivery in 1889.

The oldest valentine in existence was written in 1415.

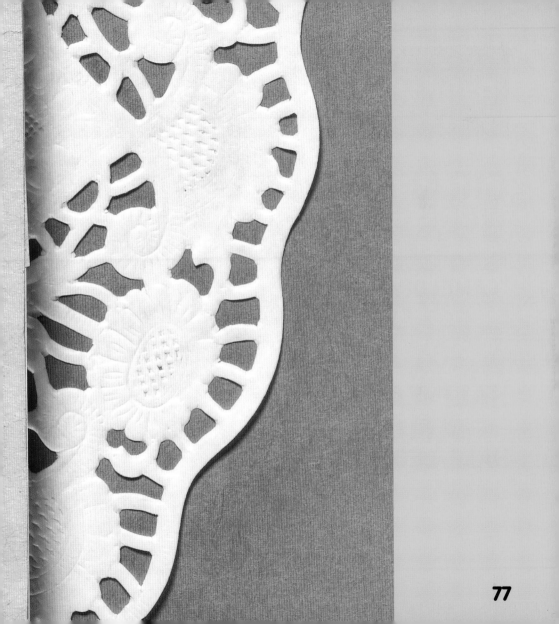

Dalmatians are born without spots.

GIRAFFES
WERE ONCE
CALLED
"CAMELOPARDS"
BECAUSE PEOPLE
THOUGHT
THEY WERE
HALF-CAMEL
~ AND ~
# HALF-LEOPARD.

Of any animal, the **pig** has a **diet** most like a human's.

THERE IS NO SOUND IN SPACE.

Couples in Finland can get married in a chapel built out of snow.

Some chickens lay green or blue eggs.

You take about 25,000 breaths every day.

The longest a person has gone without sleep is ten days.

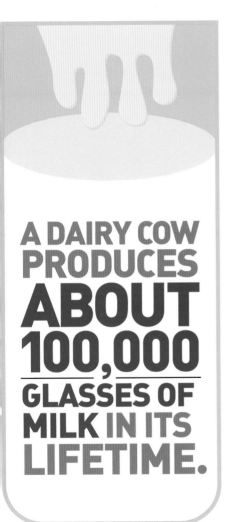

A DAIRY COW PRODUCES ABOUT 100,000 GLASSES OF MILK IN ITS LIFETIME.

Yo-yos rode on two space shuttles.

KOALAS STAY AWAKE FOR ONLY FOUR HOURS A DAY.

E·E·L·S ◄ C·A·N ◄ S·W

IT IS IMPOSSIBLE TO SNEEZE WITH YOUR EYES OPEN.

The **PRAYING MANTIS** is the only insect that can **LOOK OVER ITS SHOULDER.**

BACKWARD.

JUPITER HAS 63 MOONS.

Stretched out, your **digestive system** is nearly **30 feet long.**

(9.5 m)

Apples are one-quarter air.

Babies yawn before they are born.

Scents smell better through your

A
GROUP OF
PORCUPINES
IS CALLED A
PRICKLE.

Eating shrimp can turn white flamingos pink.

KETCHUP
was originally
SOLD AS
MEDICINE.

The average person **walks** about **80,000 miles** (128,750 km) in a lifetime.

That's more than three times around the world!

The **NORTH POLE** is **warmer than** the **SOUTH POLE.**

CATERPILLARS have mouths, but **BUTTERFLIES** don't.

Earth is the only planet not named after a **Greek or Roman god.**

You can tell lions apart by the spots at the base of their whiskers.

Hippopotomonstro

Bees visit about five million flowers to make one average-size jar of honey.

squippedaliophobia is the fear of long words.

Recycling one soda can saves a TV for three hours.

Only **MALE TOADS**

Croak.

A man **flung a coin** more than ten feet using his **earlobe as a slingshot.** (3 m)

Your tongue grows new **taste buds** about every two weeks.

THE BAHAMAS ONCE HAD AN UNDERSEA POST OFFICE.

The world's **biggest frog** IS THE SIZE OF A **house cat.**

The total **earthworm** population in the **United States** **weighs** **ten times** **more** than the total human population.

A **porcupine** can have 30,000 quills.

One **ear of corn** has about **500** kernels.

GIRAFFES
e one of the only animals **born with horns.**

Wearing a hat on your head helps warm your feet.

All cats are born with **blue eyes.**

MONKEYS CAN GO BALD IN OLD AGE, JUST LIKE HUMANS CAN.

SIX MILLION POUNDS OF
(2.7 million kg)
SPACE DUST
SETTLE ON EARTH EVERY YEAR.

A 3,000-YEAR-OLD MUMMY CAN STILL HAVE **FINGERPRINTS.**

A **snowflake** can take up to **two hours** to fall from a **cloud** to the ground.

PUMPKINS ALSO COME IN

RED, GREEN, YELLOW, BLUE, TAN, **&** WHITE.

Your skeleton

has about

300

BONES

when you are born,

but only

206

by the
time you
grow up.

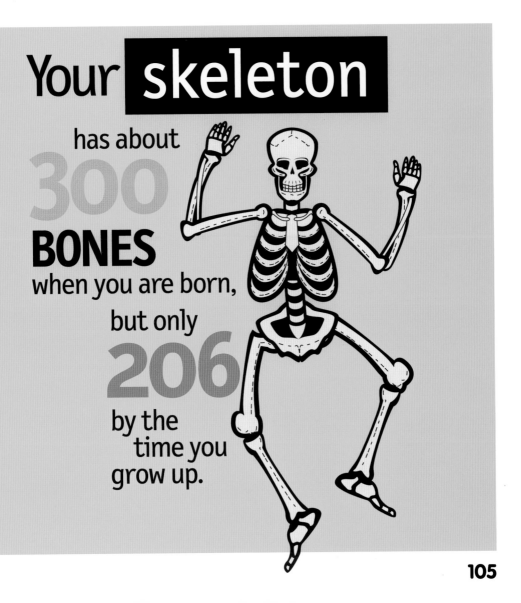

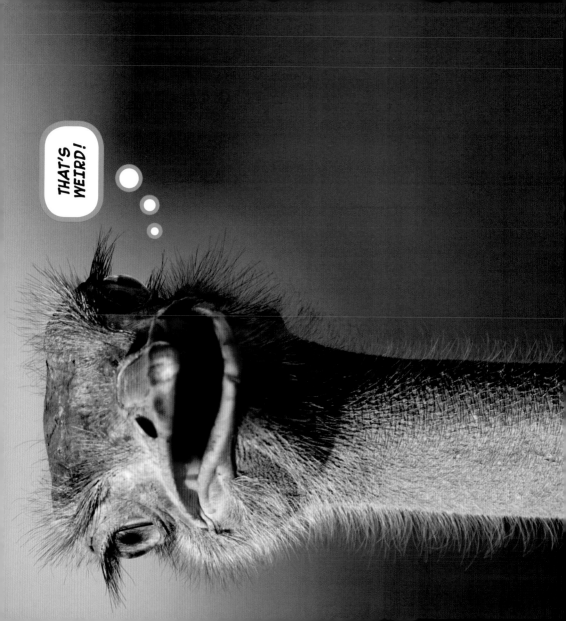

An ostrich's eye is bigger than its brain.

A LINE OF ALL THE *HARRY POTTER* BOOKS SOLD COULD CIRCLE THE EARTH TWICE.

TARANTULAS CAN LIVE FOR UP TO 20 YEARS.

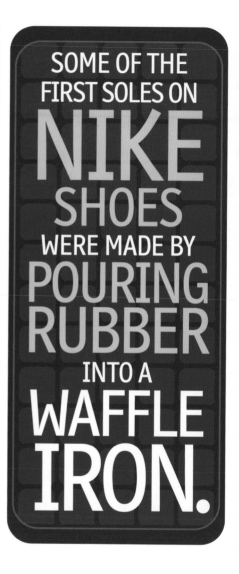

SOME OF THE FIRST SOLES ON NIKE SHOES WERE MADE BY POURING RUBBER INTO A WAFFLE IRON.

The Earth's temperature rises slightly during a full moon.

A Rubik's Cube can make
43,252,003,274,489,856,000
different **combinations.**

Popsicles **WERE INVENTED BY AN** 11-year-old.

AN *OSTRICH*
CAN RUN AS FAST AS A
RACEHORSE.

Sharks have existed **LONGER** than trees.

ONE (5 mL) TEASPOON OF SEAWATER CONTAINS FIVE MILLION LIVING ORGANISMS.

From about **March 21** to September 23 the **sun never sets** at the **North Pole.**

More
than
200
people
could fit
inside the
world's
biggest
igloo.

Winter
lasts for
21 years
on Uranus

100 FEET LONG. (31 m)

Most
squid
have three hearts.

ASTRONAUTS **GROW** — UP TO — 3 INCHES (76 mm) **TALLER** IN OUTER **SPACE.**

Jupiter weighs **twice as MUCH** as all the other planets in our **solar system** combined.

ABOUT

75

PERCENT

OF ALL

VOLCANOES

ARE

UNDERWATER.

118

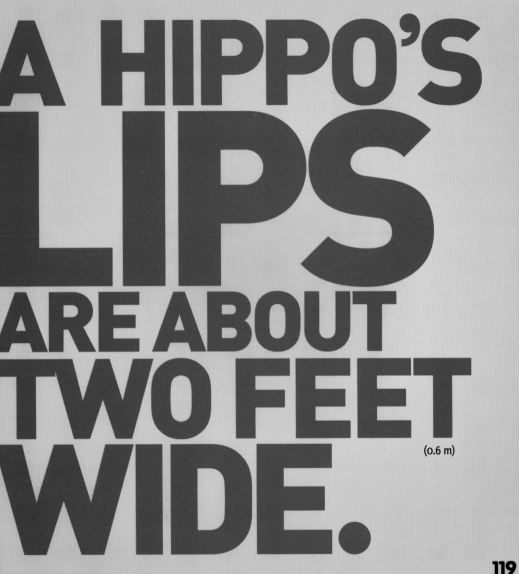

A HIPPO'S LIPS ARE ABOUT TWO FEET WIDE.

(0.6 m)

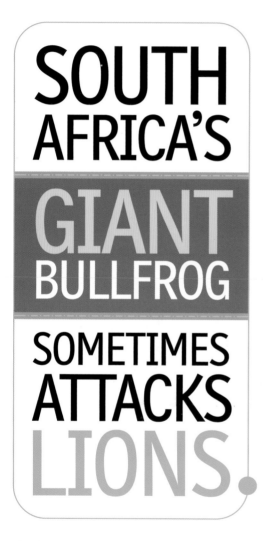

SOUTH AFRICA'S GIANT BULLFROG SOMETIMES ATTACKS LIONS.

If you weigh **50 pounds** (23 kg) **on Earth,** you would weigh about **3 pounds** (1.4 kg) **on Pluto.**

ONLY **MALE TURKEYS GOBBLE; FEMALES CLICK.**

It would take about

788,832,000

two-inch yellow
(5 cm)

sticky notes

to encircle the globe.

OYSTERS CHANGE FROM MALE TO FEMALE.

A space suit costs about ten million dollars.

elephants

Without clothes, you would start to feel cold at **77°F.**

(25°C)

The world's first **underwater hotel** is in Key Largo, Florida.

...can use their trunks as snorkels.

Fish can't close their eyes.

Detached
sea star
arms
sometimes grow
new >>>>
bodies.

Your eyes produce a teaspoon of tears (5 mL) every hour.

When you have lived for 2.4 billion seconds, you will be 75 years old.

Originally carrots were purple, not orange.

1,000,000,000,000,000 (that's one quadrillion) **ants** live on Earth.

8,962 people made snow angels at the **same time** on the grounds of the North Dakota State Capitol in the U.S.A.

The flag of every **country** in the world has at least one of the five colors in the **Olympic rings:** blue, yellow, **black,** green, **and red.**

HAWAII IS MOVING ABOUT THREE INCHES CLOSER TO JAPAN EVERY YEAR.

(7.6 cm)

About
150,000 hairs
are growing on your head
right now.

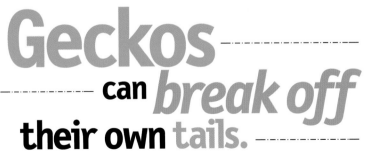

Geckos ————
———— can *break off*
their own tails. ————

A litter of kittens is also called a **kindle.**

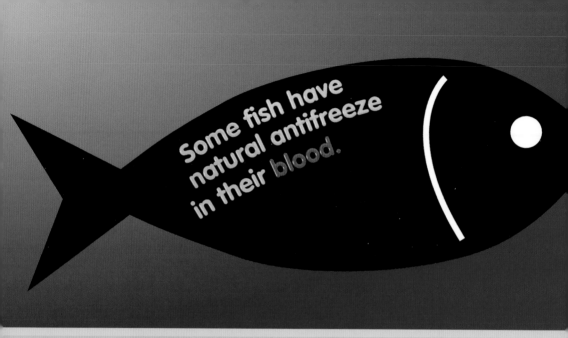

Some fish have natural antifreeze in their blood.

HUMANS AND SLUGS SHARE MORE THAN HALF OF THEIR GENES.

Alligator's eggs hatch male babies in hot temperatures and female babies in cooler temperatures.

Astronomers have discovered a star that is made of a 10-billion-trillion-trillion-carat diamond.

A head of **broccoli** is made up of **hundreds of small flower** buds.

A storm
on Neptune was as wide as...

the entire
Earth.

Chewing **gum** can make your heart beat **faster.**

A 158-year-old **holiday card** was auctioned off in the U.K. for nearly **£22,250** (about $35,000) in 2001.

The **surface** of the Atlantic Ocean is **saltier** than the surface of the **Pacific Ocean.**

The
50 tallest
mountains
in the world
are all in
Asia.

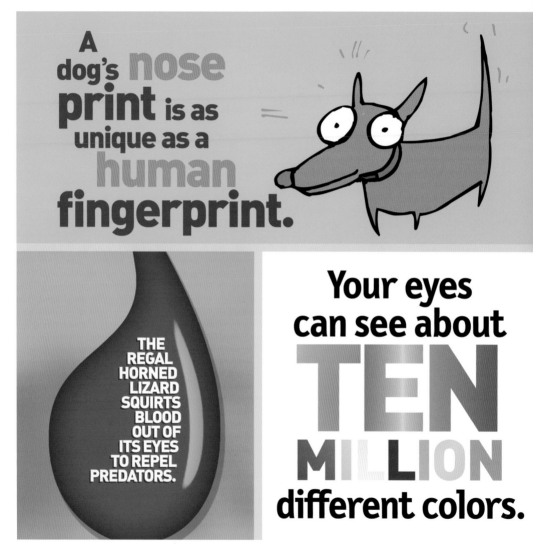

A dog's **nose print** is as unique as a **human fingerprint.**

THE REGAL HORNED LIZARD SQUIRTS BLOOD OUT OF ITS EYES TO REPEL PREDATORS.

Your eyes can see about TEN MILLION different colors.

Didaskaleinophobia

is the fear of going to school.

The **lowest known temperature** on Earth **(-128.6°F)** (-89.2°C) was recorded in **Antarctica.**

Ancient Egyptians took up to 70 days to make a mummy.

BEFORE TOOTHPASTE WAS INVENTED, SOME PEOPLE CLEANED THEIR TEETH WITH CHARCOAL.

The **Great Wall of China** spans roughly **4,500 miles**— (7,240 km) that's almost as long as the continent of **Africa.**

URP!

SHEEP BURPS CONTRIBUTE TO GLOBAL WARMING.

The heaviest known lobster weighed **44.6** pounds.

(20.2 kg)

September begins on the same day of the week as December every year.

A WOMAN IN CALIFORNIA, U.S.A., REMEMBERS ALMOST EVERY DAY OF HER LIFE...

SINCE SHE WAS 11.

Tyrannosaurus rex means "tyrant lizard king" in Latin.

GRRR!

146

The **sun** has enough **energy** to burn for **100 billion** more years.

A swordfish can swim...

**about as fast as
a cheetah can run.**

A BOWLING PIN HAS TO TILT ABOUT TEN DEGREES

TO FALL DOWN.

A PENNSYLVANIA BAKERY MADE

The hottest stars are blue.

SCIENTISTS BELIEVE THAT SATURN'S RINGS WILL EVENTUALLY DISAPPEAR.

(16 m)

OT DOG THAT WAS 54 FEET LONG.

It would take a stack of **more than nine Empire State Buildings** to equal the average depth of the ocean.

The "**barking pigeon**" has a call that sounds like a **loud dog.**

SAND melts at around **3000°F.**

(1649°C)

ALL OF TODAY'S PET HAMSTERS CAN BE TRACED BACK TO **ONE HAMSTER FAMILY** THAT LIVED IN **SYRIA** IN 1930.

A CAT'S TOP SPEED IS ABOUT

31 MILES AN HOUR.
(50 km)

The largest **spider** in the world is wider than a **basketball.**

371,000 is the average number of people **born** every day.

The oldest bat fossil ever found was **50 million years old.**

When **bald eagles** were named, the word **"bald"** meant **"white."**

There is real **GOLD** in the sun.

Humans **blink** about **17,000 times a day.**

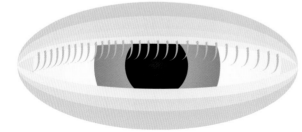

GLASS CAN LAST FOR MILLIONS OF YEARS ON EARTH.

THE LONGEST GAME OF MONOPOLY PLAYED IN A TREE HOUSE LASTED

286

HOURS.

Some **giant jellyfish** have **tentacles** that could **stretch** more than the length of a basketball **court.**

About 12,000 animal crackers are created every minute.

About one-tenth of the Earth's surface is covered in ice.

Houseflies buzz in

A QUICK-HANDED PERFORMER TWISTED 747 BALLOON SCULPTURES IN 1 HOUR.

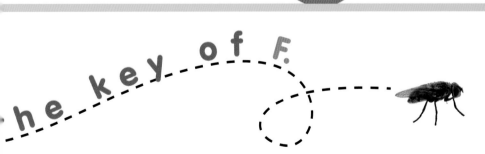

he key of F.

The **air** trapped inside an **iceberg** can be **thousands of years old.**

You have to climb a 293-step spiral staircase to reach the top of the Leaning Tower of Pisa.

Chickens
see daylight
45 minutes
before humans do.

A giant squid's eyeball can be as **big** as a human head.

There's a one in a trillion chance that a piece of space junk will land on your house today.

YOU CAN **CALL HOME** FROM AN **ICE** TELEPHONE BOOTH AT A FESTIVAL IN **ALASKA,** U.S.A.

THE WORLD'S TINIEST SEAHORSE IS SMALLER THAN A POSTAGE STAMP.

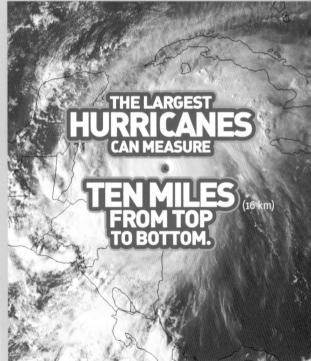

THE LARGEST **HURRICANES** CAN MEASURE **TEN MILES** (16 km) **FROM TOP TO BOTTOM.**

The largest salamanders can grow as long as bicycles.

A Canadian juice company made a 195-gallon (738 L) fruit smoothie that could have filled four bathtubs.

Apes laugh when tickled.

If you spent **a dollar** every second, it would take **about 32 years** to spend a **billion dollars**

DOLPHINS SLEEP WITH ONE EYE OPEN.

An octopus can have nearly **2,000 suckers** on its arms.

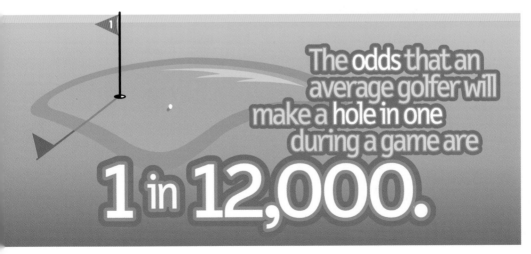

The odds that an average golfer will make a **hole in one** during a game are **1 in 12,000.**

Earth
travels about
1.6 MILLION
MILES
(2.6 million km)
every day.

AN ALLIGATOR GROWS ABOUT **3,000 TEETH** IN A LIFETIME.

MANATEES ARE RELATED TO **ELEPHANTS.**

A 14-pound
(6.4 kg)
pearl was found
in a giant
clam.

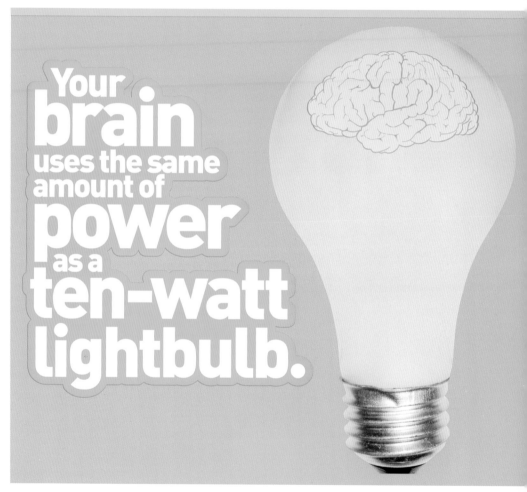

Your **brain** uses the same amount of **power** as a **ten-watt lightbulb.**

THERE ARE MORE TEXT MESSAGES SENT EACH DAY THAN THERE ARE PEOPLE ON EARTH.

A cornflake shaped like the U.S. state of Illinois sold for **$1,350.**

Saturn is made partly of **helium**—the same gas used to fill party balloons.

Most pirates never buried their loot.

A gold nugget found in California, U.S.A., weighed a whopping 160 pounds—about as much as 12 bowling balls.

(72.6 kg)

Kangaroos lick their forearms to stay cool.

Your **ears** produce more **wax** when you're **afraid.**

YOUR **HEARTBEAT** IS SO POWERFUL THAT IT COULD **SHOOT WATER** SIX FEET (1.8 m) INTO THE AIR.

Nomads created **ice skates** made of **bone** at least **4,000 years ago.**

The **Queen** of **England** has a **crown studded** with more than **3,000** precious gems.

A *Tyrannosaurus rex* fossil was sold to a museum for more than eight million dollars.

The **binturong,** a southeast Asian mammal, smells like **buttered popcorn** when excited.

A cave in Croatia, has a 1,683-foot-deep pit, the **deepest hole on Earth.**

(513 m)

A snake can **eat prey** that is **twice the width** of its head.

A group of **sea otters** is called a raft.

The offspring of a whale and a dolphin is a **wholphin.**

650 HOUSE-FLIES weigh less than **ONE OUNCE** (28 g)

A rattlesnake's **rattle** is made of the same material as your fingernails.

A mouse's heart is shorter than a Tic Tac

Liquids floating in outer space become sphere-shaped.

A seahorse can move its eyes in opposite directions.

A HUMAN EYELASH LASTS APPROXIMATELY THREE TO FIVE MONTHS.

189

An **eagle** can spot a rabbit from more than a **mile** (1.6 km) away.

Forest fires can travel faster uphill than downhill.

Mice can have up to 105 babies a year.

MORE THAN TWO MILLION ANIMA

A **sand castle** in **Maine, U.S.A.** stood as **high** as a three-story building.

Y IN AIRPLANES EVERY YEAR.

Peaches and almonds are related.

A **56**-LEAF CLOVER WAS DISCOVERED IN JAPAN.

A red flag was a symbol for battle in ancient Rome.

A **newborn koala** is about the size of a **jelly bean.**

THE WORD PURPLE COMES FROM A GREEK WORD FOR A TYPE OF SHELLFISH

197

The highest known **jump** by a **pig** is 27.5 inches— (69.9 cm) that's the height of a St. Bernard!

THAT'S REALLY WEIRD!

Toe wrestling
is a competitive sport.

FACTFINDER

Illustrations are indicated by **boldface.**

FACTFINDER

FACTFINDER

Since 1888, the National Geographic Society has funded more than 12,000 research, exploration, and preservation projects around the world. The Society receives funds from National Geographic Partners, LLC, funded in part by your purchase. A portion of the proceeds from this book supports this vital work. To learn more, visit www.natgeo.com/info.

For more information, visit www.nationalgeographic.com, call 1-800-647-5463, or write to the following address:
National Geographic Partners, LLC
1145 17th Street NW
Washington, D.C. 20036-4688 U.S.A.

Staff for this Book
Robin Terry, *Project Editor*
Eva Absher, *Art Direction and Design*
Lori Epstein, *Illustrations Editor*
Jo Tunstall, *Research*
Grace Hill, *Associate Managing Editor*
Lewis R. Bassford, *Production Manager*
Susan Borke, *Legal and Business Affairs*

Based on the "Weird But True" department in
NATIONAL GEOGRAPHIC KIDS magazine
Jülide Obuz Dengel, Jonathan Halling,
  Nicole Lazarus, *Designers*
Robin Terry, *Senior Editor*
Kelley Miller, Jay Sumner, *Photo Editors*
Erin Monroney, Sharon Thompson, *Writer-Researchers*
Marilyn Terrell, Mridula Srinivasan, Jeffrey Wandel,
  Erin Whitmer, *Freelance Researchers*

Manufacturing and Quality Management
Christopher A. Liedel, *Chief Financial Officer*
Phillip L. Schlosser, *Vice President*
Chris Brown, *Technical Director*
Rachel Faulise, *Manufacturing Manager*
Nicole Elliott, *Manufacturing Manager*

Visit us online:
Kids: nationalgeographic.com/kids
Parents: nationalgeographic.com
Teachers: nationalgeographic.com/education
Librarians: ngchildrensbooks.org

For information about special discounts for bulk purchases, please contact National Geographic Books Special Sales: ngspecsales@ngs.org

For rights or permissions inquiries, please contact National Geographic Books Subsidiary Rights: ngbookrights@ngs.org

Library of Congress Cataloging-in-Publication Data

Weird but true! 2 : 300 outrageous facts.
    p. cm.
  Includes index.
  ISBN 978-1-4263-0688-4 (pbk. : alk. paper)
  1. Curiosities and wonders--Juvenile literature. I. National Geographic Society (U.S.) II. Weird but true.
  AG243.W38 2010
  001.9--dc22

                                    2010004809

Printed in China
16/PPS/4-BX

YOU LOVE

everything WEIRD and WACKY, right?

So check out these **HILARIOUS** fill-in-the-_____
noun
storybooks, created by and starring **YOU!**

Did you know that **dolphins sleep** with one eye open, or that **meteorites** the size of **basketballs land on Earth** about once a month?

The creators of NATIONAL GEOGRAPHIC KIDS, the nation's most popular kids' magazine, bring you the next exciting edition of this blockbuster series!

300 more amazing facts that are almost too strange to believe.

Even wilder, wackier trivia about animals, **outer space,** amazing feats, food, pets, toys, geography, money, weather, and more!

Every page contains even more **mind-bending fun!**

Check out the other books in the Weird But True series!

DOWNLOAD

the NEW *National Geographic Kids Weird But True* for iPhone®, iPod touch®, and iPad®!

kids.nationalgeographic.com

$7.95 U.S./$8.95 CAN/£5.99 UK

ISBN 978-1-4263-0688-4 /Printed in China

5 0 7 9 5

9 781426 306884